MW01275728

The Art of Clipping One's Nails

The Fool and the Wind

Michael Angelo Megla

Editorial Dos Islas

The Art of Clipping One's Nails

The Fool and the Wind

First Edition, 2020

Editor: Odalys Interian

Cover Design: Amanda Lorenzo

© Michael Angelo Megla

© Editorial Dos Islas, 2020

ISBN: 9798667650584

Editorial Dos Islas

Miami-Vancouver 2020

The Art of Clipping One's Nails

The Fool and the Wind

Michael Angelo Megla

The Art of Clipping One's Nails

The Art of Clipping One's Nails is a book that carries that unique quality found in rivers, there is a sound in it; that "flowing liquidity" that is rare, and only present in good poetry.

Michael's poetry shook me. I was taken aback by the multiplicity of songs and voices within, there is an immediate calling in Michael that ruptures the senses with its force of words and images, there's an almost painful honesty that captivates, there is a current, a torrent that is Michael Megla when he exercises this calling from within. It compels, for when one reads this young author, one feels from the start the presence of an enlivened verse, a live water, like a flow emanating from the poems, and this flow, this force creates an "entity" that stands free in its own right, among the pages.

That unit, that "it" is the poet's voice. Despite his young age, Michael Megla's unique and wise lyrics let us roam freely in a deep, inner world, which reveals to the poetry lover that Megla is a poet reminiscing Blake, Frost, and some of the Zen masters. His poetic voice constitutes a standalone metaphor of these times. It carries great pain and energy. And by this I mean, he gives us the gift of a highly philosophical verse, one that compels to feel he himself is the abyss, he is poem, and when he becomes his poems, they are submarine inhabitants of the author's dissimilar, inner worlds; fishes of the great abyssal depths, swimming in the midst with Death, Love, Life, and the whole of creation, fishes breeding with the futility of passing, intertwined with the infallible, yet inconsequential mark of our presence in the universe. Herein, a direct poet, indeed! He who becomes word, Megla wields imageries with an innate force that compels one like a beast, sending us to the depths to look at life in the face, to ask of her the answer to our most fundamental question, what is life itself. As if the images were amulets which the soul clings to in desperation, and armed with all the questions and answers, he puts them outright, he wears them like a crest, he allows us but a glimpse into the poets "mundos", and "trasmundos", going from the highest peaks of thinking, he lets us into the gates of Depths; we become trespassers into the world of "the Fool", (as Megla calls himself) for we too, as the poet compels, shall see life for what it is; a Passing, a fleeting state of being, a stone on our way which was made by our own doings, a learning and failure of the mastery of the art of washing one's bowl; another beautiful metaphor. An allegory that came to the poet while preforming such a mundane task made into a poem, this in my view, constitutes magnificent, innovative poetry.

With great mastery of the haiku and the koan, Michael enters nature, becomes a tree, speaks to a beloved valley, or decides to go "grassing", raining, "universing" (the poets' own term). In other poems he acknowledges the profound importance that entails assuming Sadness as a potential friend, an essential state of being, understanding it as another "flow" of the river, of the water, of Death. He tells us the way is accepting finitude as the infinite, he embraces Loneliness as an equal, as an essential cloak the true poet wears, for it is right in there he dwells, it is the modus operandi of the poet who is, by choice, committed to his time.

I here then, leave you with these poems, these artifacts, these fishes in a reverie of verses. May they take you high and low, like they took me, raining, grassing, living, fooling, dying, "universing", as we keep trying to live and learn, that graceful yet intricate "Art of Clipping One's Nails".

Lidice Megla

(Author, Translator & Poet) Canmore, June 27th, 2020

For my family, and for the wind in the trees; it is thanks to them both I can write such beautiful nonsense.

The Wise
>   For Peaches.

Fastened by fear we cling to faith,

deaf to the wise who whisper,

Let go...

Naked and afraid we smile at steel,

never heeding the wise who say,

Let go...

Love quickens our heart's pace,

as we shut away the few smiles we keep,

the wise cry to us unheard,

Let go...

The child's mind goes numb,

brought to a feverish pitch of sought out pleasure

The blind push on, followed closely by the dumb

The words of the wise go drowned in the waters of ecstasy,

Let go...

The wise trouble themselves,

forever seeking to right what is wrong

Who is left now to remind them,

Let go...

Michael Megla

The Crow's Song

See me for I have made,

the image of myself fashioned in clay

Nor for night or blessed day,

can make me see the song we play

Our notes flee the world below,

solace only to the faithful crow

His cry rings the joke of death,

our lies he bears upon his crest

Regret rests in its deepest waters,

guilt nestles into its darkest corners

So flees does the crow,

And see

how he carries love aloft his wings,

With death sunken in one claw,

and life clasped in the other

Beholden to illusion, mesmerized does he fly,

From his pitched beak

the notes do cry,

life is love for the hope that we die.

The Same

See the water how it flows,

the very same way the winds blows,

the very same way does cry the crow,

only he who sees without looking,

who touches without coveting,

will feel the divinity in all.

For through winter to fall,

comes purpose to call.

Become what you will,

see what you will.

Love the wind,

treasure the stone,

for despite what you see,

and what is thought to be sane,

the wind, stone, and you are all one in the same.

Michael Megla

Pattern

The patterns flow and squeeze

ever changing in the cosmic breeze,

Blood and love flow in equal measure,

the keys to existence's fateful treasure,

The secret that very few hold,

To no longer freeze, go with the cold.

Blank Pages

Listening to crows,

I stare at a blank page,

Laughing all the while at my world's cage,

For despite what I love and my eye that I see,

I'm no more than a fool, and he is with me.

Simple Pleasures

The simplest of pleasures,

Are the most complex of measures,

Dream to forget:

That the fool within is not easily met.

Flower's Gaze

A flower's gaze is one hard to hold,

For its secret I know can never be told.

But how I wish to shout it to the world from my fool's cave:

The world is exactly what I and you have made.

Michael Megla

A Spot of Nihilism

For Father.

Burn the Bibles,

Kill the Gods,

Destroy all notion of favour and fame,

For none are needed to hear the sound of the rain.

The Monster Within

A monster that dreams,

sleeps by any means,

only to wake up in cold fury,

in freezing vengeance,

it spills the blood we find so alluring.

Never seen, we catch glimpses,

ripping my mind, it minces.

The evil in laughter,

the joy in rancor,

run or hide,

dread the coming of the tide.

Too late had I turned to see,

the monster that sleeps, in my eyes takes hold of me.

The strength of a shadow,

rends my hallowed bone.

The dark does sleep,

death glaring into the eyes of the weak.

Yet it is those most frail,

whose deathly power does entail,

23

the kindness of an end,

and the cruelty of a begging.

The reaper comes to take my hand,

a jovial friend,

Only now do I see,

the sting of his brand.

Eyes

What do I see in my eyes?

is it me or your disguise?

Do I see my I?

Or perhaps it is my eye that sees me.

Too long to know,

Too soon to forget,

A deepest friend I've never met.

Another could never breath,

had I not known he wasn't me,

Do I need you to be free?

Is it me or my name that bleeds?

Too long to know

Too soon to forget,

The deepest is always the final breath.

For it is too long to know,

but too soon to forget,

That death bear's life's crest.

And should death begin anew,

perhaps the one I see in the mirror, is you.

Michael Megla

Obsession

I can see you,

in the depths of toil,

in the life of a seed,

I see you born anew.

Take my mangled hand, and with obsessive thrill,

a crippled visage of what was once human will.

Blind to love, not a care for hate,

numbing cold becomes my telling brand.

Alone now do I sit,

thy covetous image comes calling,

screeching my name in ecstatic horror,

living my failing, too painful to admit.

Begone from my soul's freezing,

what my blood would give,

to have what my flesh does crave.

A burning of disease, a break of breathing.

Your shadow haunts my steps,

it becomes sinful to rest,

my blood of dust and sinew of ash,

stain the streets of shining gold,

and taint the painting of being.

Too long to know,

too soon to forget,

perhaps all I need is the easing of death.

Michael Megla

Streets of Gold

I walk in the streets of gold,

my flesh matching the steel and silver cold.

The earth turns to ash and wind,

the trees to a shining cage,

full of strangers, all blindingly afraid,

of idle hands and insightful souls

How we love to burn the world of old.

The sheen of greed splits our hands,

calloused and bruised,

we build the roads of gold.

Yet for all their shine and weight,

they lead to nothing and they mean nothing, but fear and eyes closed.

Nothing lives but for our reflection on the streets of fire,

how is it that we are the objects of our desire?

Empty smiles and hollow eyes creep, ever further from the secret we keep

No matter how lusting for gold,

he who is alive does love,

for it staves off his steel and silver cold.

Alone
> *For Shelly*

I awake in the morning,

the cold clinging to my unawakened bones

Dew glistens in fleeting beauty,

I am alone.

Skies of scarlet smile, I turn away

None to love nor to be loved

On my throne I sit,

I am alone.

I awake in the morning,

the red sky turns slowly grey,

the green grass everlastingly fades

The birds smile,

I turn away,

I am alone.

A cage of grim strength gilds my skin,

All faces to grey, devoid of life, devoid of sin,

The sweetest pains turn to pitiless pleasure,

how my strength and solitude I treasure,

I am alone.

I awake in the morning,

Michael Megla

the dawn air eases my chest,

Smile all you will my sweetest friend,

but the cold I have become,

And as I sink into my throne of lifeless bones,

I am as I always have been,

tired and alone.

Bliss

So speaks the dumb:

I've got God under my thumb!

So speaks the wise:

If only God was a crumb

so I could eat him whole!

Generous kings cry:

God is on my side!

And the jester knows the king is blind.

The hunter knows only the forest,

the air is God the most.

The blind scream with glee:

vision needs not a host!

The blissful say nothing,

for in doing so, God makes something.

31

Michael Megla

Stone
>   *For Mother*

Beauty blazes in fleeting,

its flames dance in my eyes

The secret, my soul cries,

through your mind's night and day,

the stone in your way is one you've made

Purpose flowers on every tree,

through every bird my soul sings to me,

The stone in your way is one you've made

Eternity fills the air in my lungs,

my breath sings in mind shattering harmony,

The stone in your way is one you've made

Love fills my chest and burns my skin

The fear of losing myself, easing my tormented mind,

The soul whispers in a lover's embrace,

The stone in your way is one you've made.

Music plays in the soul's playful dance,

It cries to me from within,

See the world you have made,

and be not afraid,

The stone in your way is one you've made.

Michael Megla

Flame

Flames in my mind dance,

The truth: they are flaming

dances on in the night.

The sky christens my flame

Burning with the curse of man's shame;

for all our might and witless power,

who can there be but we to blame?

The Dams Our Souls Keep

The heart sings for pleasure

blind to all other measure,

but the soul craves that which does not speak

flame and water, the dams our souls do keep.

Haiku Series

Eternal Spring

A mountain grows tall

Trees of green grow like hair;

In eternal spring

The Mountain

Belief; dreams in passing,

Wind comes down from the mountain

I am at peace

Belief

In belief hides death,

Its joke chuckles with a smile

In death hides life

The Art of Blueberries

Tasting blueberries

Under the trees of pine, I sleep

The wind breathes in; out

36

Mist

Mist on the mountain

A veil of eternal spring,

Brings home to me; all

Grass
Wind fills fields of grass,

a sea of strands or water;

falls with the clear rain.

The Peak of a Man

The foot of a mountain grows tall.

The peak of a man grows short

The Dust

Spring rain washes the dust,

Birds float from tree to tree; see

The dust washes rain

Flowers

Flowers on the trees

do blossom for a day,

Though trees stand; always

37

Michael Megla

The Valley

For the Valley.

Will I ever see you again?

The valley which I love?

Will I see the pines rise higher than the sky?

And the mountains that withhold the brow of the world

My soul will return, though in body I will be far,

to swim in the rivers of crystal

and to shed those tears of diamond.

Return to me, valley of green

for never again will I return to you.

Confusion

Unknowing, I walk the streets of cold

if only we knew how to turn them to gold.

Flowers bloom in passing, the sun their call to sleep and waking,

if only we knew how to keep the in bloom, unbreaking.

Passing by I hear those who speak, yet have no thought,

How the devil loves the lie, the word which thought has wrought.

If only we knew how to tell the truth

The lies in masks kill, with fang and tooth.

See our ways of illusion,

It's God's wonderful way of confusion.

Michael Megla

Shit Brown

For Amanda.

Stop. What is it you know?

Are you in the spotlight, or in the flow?

Do you love or hate, smile or frown?

Do you say the blue sky is shit brown?

Do you see me or do I see you?

Only you can know the truth

And only we can see your lie:

you are not afraid to die.

But fear not my false prophet,

for if you fear death's pains, remember

You cannot say the sound of the rain.

A Bit of Cryptic

Hear the silence of the rain,

Discard all form and fame,

For every drop and sufferer came,

To see God, but saw he was plain.

Michael Megla

A World Most Fine

Colours blend the lines,

now I see a world so fine,

One dark and light,

The opposites bend my fright,

For through tireless nights and sleepless days I find,

The soul of the tyrant to be kind.

A Koan

Music and thought sing together

Unity is division, division is unity,

Where is your mind?

The sky is especially blue today.

Michael Megla

One to See

Form and flow rise mutually,

Oil and flame that caress the breeze,

Two sides of a coin do meet,

To agree there was never one to see.

Trees

Dharma is not.

Buddha is not.

Only water, and trees left to rot.

Michael Megla

The Koans

1.

You grow the trees

And they grow you

See not, See all

From the Buddha nature, we never fall.

2.

Drink deep.

Eat well.

Sleep in peace.

For reality is not worried in the least.

3.

A fool walks,

A sage talks,

What is an apple?

How deep the red of a ruby is.

4.

What is breath?

The wind in the trees.

What is Buddha?

The birds that sing.

The Sound of a Fist

Names chatter on,

the Buddha sits alone at a pond,

What is the sound of a fist?

The Sun's reflection, in a pool of mist.

A Strange Dialogue
> *For Sam.*

The wind whispered gently through the trees, carrying along its knowledge of time immemorial. In the temple, Pho was working. His master had set him out to arrange the sand garden, and he was sweating from concentration. Such it was for all the monks in the Zen school, toiling away at the maintaining of the Tao. Pho, however; was not a monk, he was but a gardener, and talented in the art of arranging the sand in the rock garden. It was only through his work, where he found peace. Meditation and contemplation of the divine the suffering of others drew him not. He was a simple man, the kind who, when sitting, truly sat. Or when walking, he just walked. And when gardening, he just worked, as was his natural pleasure. Though, he never wobbled, nor strayed from his first thought. Always he was at peace and certain. But he was but a gardener, and the other monks took no notice of him, for they could not see through their own contempt. The master knew much differently however, and watched Pho closely, with the attention of a tiger, and the furled brow of a god, with a glint of a joke in his eye. His beard swung fiercely in the wind as he observed Pho in his work. He suspected something... but knew, to avoid embarrassing the other monks, he must create a koan. So, he set out to do so.

The master was getting incredibly old and was soon to die. All the monks in the temple whispered among themselves, guessing who would be the successor, hoping for themselves to achieve attainment. They were not with the Tao. Pho continued his work every day, talking to the monks in a friendly way, talking of the master; and working silently and marvellously. To decide the successor to the mastership of the school, the master called all his thirty monks to the garden. Pho continued working, untroubled by their presence, though now watching simultaneously, for he was interested to see which of the monks would be chosen... and which would not. The master sat, in absolute confidence, washing his gaze over the students as though his eyes were wrought from the depths of the ocean. In a clean, strong voice he said.

"I am to die tomorrow." Some monks exclaimed, some wept. Pho smiled at the master's wisdom.

"We must see which of you is with Satori, so that he may succeed me in passing. Bring today all the people from the city, all the men women and children, for the Tao knows not of the illusions of men. I will choose thereafter." The monks set to work, sending letters, and going into the city to gather the people. A great crowd soon gathered, women and children, men young and old. All wished to attain Buddhahood. Pho watched, standing in the center of the rock garden, while the crowd dared not step onto the sacred pattern. Pho chuckled to himself at their supposed piety. The master stood in on top of the largest rock in the garden and called all to attention through his impressive silence. Soon nothing could be heard but the occasional wail of a small child, the wind in the trees, and the birds that sang in them. Pho stood, still in the center of the garden, in awe of the master.

The master drew a small golden object from his pocket. A coin, which he was very fond of, and was always seen tossing idly. He held it up for all to see, smiling mischievously, and asked.

"What is it?"

The monks looked to each other, brows frowned in deep thinking, trying hard to find a right answer. The head monk piped up.

"It is the divinity of opposites!" The master laughed, a sound clear and gentle as a stream, and threw the coin at the monk.

"That's what it is! I see perhaps there will be no successor. I will pass, and you will all go home." The master locked eyes with Pho, awaiting action. Pho picked up a small rock and threw it square at the master. The master moved out of its path with the ease of wind. Again, he

49

laughed like a child, this time his joy was joined by Pho's rumbling laugh.

Pho cried, amidst tears of laughter, "There it is!" And he was enlightened.

Who's Got My Mind?

The master sat gazing over his mountain pass. His temple perched above the town below, amidst snow and jagged stone. Though the cold bothered him not. Once a gardener, he was the new master, and was becoming old once more, just like his own teacher. He sat ever gracefully, tending to a small personal rock garden. A young student, no more than thirteen, was walking up the steps for a question with the master. The master smiled kindly; he had seen this sight so many times before, the Tao in disguise drifting up the stairway. The student sat next to the master. Both said nothing for a long moment. The student's face was buried in worry, preoccupied with his own mind. The master only smiled at the cold.

"Master?" The student looked to the master with enormous eyes filled with youth and curiosity, bursting with a playful light.

"Yes Tzin Sue?" The master turned his peaceful gaze over to the student.

"Please, help me to get my mind back, I have lost it! I cannot find my thoughts, and I lose sight of the Buddha Nature, the tathagata." The master puzzled for a short moment, and shouted, a sound like the ringing of an enormous bell.

"Who has stolen your mind?"....

"Well, no one, master..." And Tzin Sue was enlightened.

Michael Megla

It is Still with You

The old master walked up the temple mountain to visit his old friend, the sage. The sage was the holiest of holy men; so embraced by nature, so loved by all was he that as he sat atop his mountain, the birds would bring him gifts, and the deer would lay beside him for warmth. The master strolled up the path, each step on air, each breath light as a feather, and deep as the ocean. He came to his old friend's spot of meditation.

"Sage, may I sit?" The sage sat with his eyes closed, cut off from the world, each of his breaths an eternity. The bird's song drifted along the wind, and the softness of the trees whispered words of wisdom to those who would listen.

"Sit and meditate with me." The sage motioned to a right patch of sunlight. The master sat, smiling comfortably and looked on at the wondrous view of the valley unfolding before him.

"It is a shame your eyes are closed dear sage. Your land is most beautiful." The sage laughed; eyes still closed.

"What lies within is much more beautiful." He answered. The master in this moment knew, the sage spoke but understood not. With pity he said nothing and enjoyed the mountain air.

Unbeknownst to the master, a bear; a friend of the sage was trundling along the path. It startled the master, and so he screamed, as most would at the sight of a monstrous bear. The sage only laughed and said.

"I see it is still with you!" The master chuckled gently; a sound fresh as spring.

52

"I suppose so."

Later, after a long while of talking and laughter, the sage went into his cave to make dinner for himself and his guest. And the master, in a joke, took out his knife and carved the symbol for 'Buddha' on the sage's stone perch. When the sage returned, he went to sit, but hesitated when he saw the symbol on his seat.

"Ha! I see it is still with you!"

Michael Megla

Two Thieves

Two thieves walked past each other on a road, one going to the sea, the other to the mountain wilds. One each recognized the other and laughed both like a child.

"Where are you going with an expression so mild?"

"I go to visit a friend, the sky and his child."

"Indeed, I know them well, I myself am going to visit my wife of the depths, hell."

"Indeed, I know her well! For I am also a husband and my thirst for love does she also quell."

"I will tell her of you. Tell the sky and his child on my behalf, for I am also his wife and other craft."

Both laughed and were silent in enjoying the wind's silence.

"Who are you?"

"What a stupid question. Who is asking?"

"I am the art of having blue skies!"

"What beautiful nonsense! Look on and see me!" The thief then took what gold he was carrying and ate it whole.

"There I am you see? Now take our golden wisdom and flee!"

And the thieves two became one,

And like a breath of music lightly strung,

Became the fool,

Whose hour became his greatest tool.

Family of Faith

Hope breathes life;

Its brother despair, readies his knife;

Faith sees his children with a laugh in his eye;

and his wife, mystery, claims all when they die.

Dream on in sweet slumber, for tomorrow drinks from his cup anew;

seeing happily, that he is you.

Yesterday eyes tomorrow with food of falsehood, for he is comfortable,

and tomorrow sits, untouchable.

I sit amidst this family of mine, only to see,

I am all that could be.

And what is to find,

that which can give and take; kill and live?

I never lost it, and never found it.

The family where they sit, sing their hymn.

Breathe and die, flow or stay, stand or sit.

But either get off the pot or shit. :)

Michael Megla

All shall be gone

Dreams and thoughts in passing, no memory of where they are from.

Trees and stone, water and fire; no whispers of whence they came.

Ideals and morals, great edifices of stone thought, all notions of fortune and fame.

Cling to me, myself, and I;

For it is my game to pretend the self is alive.

I have forgotten the songs of the water, and the voice of the wind;

and it smiles at me, I shall be gone in its grin.

Faith of the soul, anger of the hypocrite, all, and all, shall be gone;

No notion will there be, of where they came from.

And in days not yet alive they will see;

our greatness, how we stood, is delusional glee.

Fear not death, for he too shall flee,

with the ring of a foolish man's song.

When all shall be gone, who will be to blame?

None but us and the wind, for we are that which we wish upon,

All, forever, shall be gone.

Beautiful Nonsense

It's raining on the grassing,

The grassing is housing the bugging,

The bugging is seeing the sunning,

and avoiding the raining,

Raining, bugging, sunning,

Universing.

Michael Megla

Dreaming

The dream blazes with untouchable light,

scaring away the stupid in the night;

Blind to it are the intelligent,

deaf to it are the wise;

The reason of man brings its demise.

Breathing the dream, leavening the dough, plowing the fields;

rain and snow falling on my hat as I come walking,

snow and wind fearing nothing as a twinkle in my eye comes winking,

My eye watches my eye, unblinking.

The dream burns with a loving flame,

laying waste to favour and fame;

Blind to it are the virtuous,

deaf to it are the holy, and the sinner;

For the dreaming is nothing, forever growing.

Music drowns the song,

Art hides the sight,

The sword kills the fight.

The dream blows with the cold wind;

stoning, peopling, dreaming, Universing.

Bring me my dream, the thinking of breathing,

the knowing of unknowing;

The cold of the flame,

The stone of the mind;

All circling to showing me,

I am what is finding,

And I am dreaming my dreaming.

Michael Megla

It

It fills my spoon,

And comes calling at noon;

It waters my drink,

And thoughts my think;

It joys my happiness,

And glooms my sadness;

It whispers in the trees,

It sings in songs,

It flames my fire,

And freezes the ice.

What is it?

Look on and see it twice, in the winding blow,

Why do you want to know?

A Little

We need just a little raining

to shoo away the flaming.

We need a little living

to shoo away the laughing.

And a little laughing to shoo away the living.

We need a little loving

to shoo away the hating.

We need a little Universing

to shoo away the humaning.

And a little humaning to shoo away the Universing.

We need just a little something

to shoo away the nothing.

We need a little dreaming

to shoo away the waking.

And a little lightning

to shoo away the darkening.

We all need just a little being

to shoo away the leaving.

Michael Megla

Don't You See?

Isn't it hard to see,

I am the trees?

Isn't it easy to see

I'm not me?

Isn't is hard to see

my eyes are the sun?

Isn't it easy to see

I am a body, and a body is me?

Isn't it hard to see

I am a gun?

And how easy it is to see

It's all for fun?

How hard is it to feel it,

It's you and you're it;

How easy it is to know

That the earth is part of your hand?

And how hard is it really,

To hear the sound of one hand?

A Little Fish

Born; and suddenly dying,

Living; and suddenly breathing,

Breathing; and suddenly thinking,

Thinking, thinking, dreaming and dreaming,

Through life we flow as a river

Never stopping

Never freeing.

Grasp all you wish,

but God is a slippery little fish.

Michael Megla

My Friend the Fool

What a lovely fool,

Who preaches like a tool,

Dream on precious fellow,

For life is good, and the sun is mellow,

The wind carries us in arms most gentle,

and you and I breathe and whisper, all is mental,

All is void,

All is nameless,

All is formless,

All is.

The Art of Clipping One's Nails

The art of clipping one's nails;

Is all the world entails,

Dream on my sweet eye,

do not be afraid, for together, we will die.

Gone forever, a gust of dust and the smell of musk;

Worry not, for what we give; is always given to us.

My sweet name; fear not your lack of favour or fame,

for in the eyes of the dreamer;

you are always the gleamer.

Behind the mask, who is there?

Who is it that's who?

Who is?

A knock comes on the door; an old friend to tell you,

be silent my sweet eye; you're it.

Michael Megla

The Art of Washing Your Bowl

My sweet eye,

Eat for it makes you whole;

Drink deep, for life takes its toll,

When the reaper comes to ask you:

Did you wash your bowl?

My dearest seeker;

Pause not for hope of certainty,

For the reaper comes to ask:

Did you wash your bowl?

Dream not of dreaming cheerfully,

For the reaper comes whispering:

Did you wash your bowl?

Chase not pictures,

For meaning lies in water pitchers;

And the reaper comes smiling:

Did you wash your bowl?

The Art of Dying

Live, so that you may die,

Fall, so that you may fly.

Dream so that you may waken,

And the birds fall away in their making.

Eat so that you may starve,

And drink so that you'll be parched.

Be stone,

So that you might be water,

Now forget you are either,

And live through that nine to fiver.

Force what comes alone,

And you will never see past my dreamy tone.

For all that I practice is this:

Die, so that you may live.

Michael Megla

A Spider on the Window

A spider dances to my music;

All eight legs jigging along,

Catching, walking; seeing through eight eyes,

What a marvelous mask,

For a God in disguise.

Music on the wind makes the trees dance;

It's easy to see at a glance,

But you'll miss it if you stare,

There is too much of it in the air;

Too much to carry a spider's care.

Seed of Evil

The art of being a seed of evil;

Goes with the soul of any good man.

The soul of good man loves its hate,

And loves its fate.

For the greatest of goods is in fact to see,

the devil in all his wisdom, is in me.

Michael Megla

Grows

Rain drops on the window;

Telling you something you can't know

Like grass, the water grows.

Leaves fall, with nothing to show.

Ask, and I will say nothing.

Sing, and I will be humming.

Move, and I will be still.

Rain falls on the window,

Speaking that which you already know;

The water, like the grass; grows.

Nothing

What is nothing,

But something?

What is knowledge,

But lies?

Truth hides in a lie,

Being firmly on the ground will help you fly.

Faith hides in non-belief

Smooth and uncaring,

Dreams whisper to us from underneath.

Come with me to lead you by the hand;

To see there was nothing to hold;

And to lead, there is no man.

Michael Megla

Forget

Forget thy name.

Seek not to share your blame,

or hold others to shame.

Forget thy name.

Forget thy words.

Speak only the truth and you will find,

you walk among sheep and countless herds.

Forget thy wolf and lion, but be not overly kind,

For pity without truth is shame.

Forget thy words.

Forget thy wisdom.

Dream not of words of admiration for words of flow,

Seek not forbidden truths of the crow.

Look instead to be wind and water,

the soul and mind.

Burn hot thy soul's fire,

and forget thy wisdom.

Forget thine eyes,

for with them, not of them do you see.

72

Cold is the man who cuts the world with his eyes,

and deeply does he seek to cut into thee.

Seek not thine eyes for you look not for me.

Forget thy grasping love

for only in seeking love will you lose it.

Your lover shows truth in their lies,

and lies in their truth.

Forget thy grasping love and learn to let go in love.

Forget thy self,

for thy self cannot be known,

cannot be touched,

cannot be grown.

Forget thy self,

for it is the one thing eternally remembered.

Forget thy food,

for only the body may be fed,

remember instead the body, and your food will follow.

Forget thy world

for world is not,

life is not.

Remember the thoughtless, the world-less, and light will follow.

Michael Megla

Forget thy world.

Forget thy music,

for silent winds sing to you,

and breathe the harmony of un-harmony.

Forget thy silence and music,

for the wind gently hums a tune.

We've but to forget and listen.

Thus, I forget, and one day on death's bed, I will remember.

Who?

Who's got your mind?

Can you not see you, or are you blind?

Love for the dream makes one wise,

But too much love covers one in lies.

Where is your captor, you who would be free?

See him there and flee!

The captor is you, and you are him,

And the greatest trick of all,

There is none to fall!

Where is your mind?

Look on, it's there!

For in seeking you have already found a mind most fair.

Michael Megla

Blank

I'll be quite frank,

The wisest book,

Is blank.

Michael Megla (2001, St. Albert, AB. Canada) is a young poet and writer, who has always believed in the spirit of the word. Writing is both a pastime and a means of expression for this handsome devil of a man. Having lived in many places already around the world and seen many things, with exquisite sense of humour, and mastery of the verse, Michael uses both the internal and external world to craft his foolish imagery, while he shares his unique views and innovative poetry with us

Manufactured by Amazon.ca
Bolton, ON

19049587R00046